TODAY'S SUPERSTARS

Maria Sharapova

By Mark Stewart

Gareth Stevens Publishing

Please visit our web site at www.garethstevens.com.
For a free catalog describing Gareth Stevens Publishing's list of high-quality books,
call 1-800-542-2595 (USA) or 1-800-387-3178 (Canada).
Gareth Stevens Publishing's fax: 1-877-542-2596

Library of Congress Cataloging-in-Publication Data
Stewart, Mark, 1960–
Maria Sharapova / by Mark Stewart.
p. cm.— (Today's superstars)
Includes bibliographical references and index.
ISBN-10: 1-4339-1967-2 ISBN-13: 978-1-4339-1967-1 (lib. bdg.)
ISBN-10: 1-4339-2160-X ISBN-13: 978-1-4339-2160-5 (soft cover)
1. Sharapova, Maria, 1987– —Juvenile literature. 2. Tennis players—Russia (Federation) Biography—Juvenile literature. 3. Women tennis players—Russia (Federation)—Biography—Juvenile literature. I. Title.
GV994.S47S747 2010
796.342092—dc22 [B] 2009004891

This edition first published in 2010 by
Gareth Stevens Publishing
A Weekly Reader® Company
1 Reader's Digest Road
Pleasantville, NY 10570-7000 USA

Executive Managing Editor: Lisa M. Herrington
Senior Designer: Keith Plechaty

Art Direction and Page Production: The Design Lab

Photo Credits: cover, title page Matthew Stockman/Getty Images; p. 4, 40 AP Photo/Anja Niedringhaus; p. 6 AP Photo/Mark J. Terrill; p. 7 Entertainment Press/Shutterstock; p. 8 AP Photo/David Vincent, File; p. 9 AP Photo/Michel Euler; p. 10 Frederic J. Brown/AFP/Getty Images; p. 12 AP Photo/Mikhail Metzel; p. 13 AP Photo/Martin Meissner; p. 14 Mashkov Yuri/ITAR-TASS/Corbis; p. 15 Michel Philippot/Sygma/Corbis; p. 16 Brian Smith/Outline/Corbis; p. 18, 46 Brian Smith/Outline/Corbis; p. 19 AP Photo/Steve Holland, File; p. 21 AP Photo/Alastair Grant; p. 22 AP Photo/Richard Drew; p. 24 AP Photo/Andrew Parsons, PA; p. 25, 46 AP Photo/Anja Niedringhaus; p. 26 AP Photo/Lynne Sladky; p. 27 Scott Halleran/Getty Images; p. 28 AP Photo/Rob Griffith; p. 30 Jason O'Brien/Icon SMI/Corbis; p. 31 Shaun Best/Reuters/Corbis; p. 32 Pavel Wolberg/epa/Corbis; p. 33 Paul Cowan/Shutterstock; p. 34, 41 AP Photo/Michelle McLoughlin; p. 36 Elsa/Getty Images; p. 37 glo/Shutterstock; p. 38 AP Photo/Jennifer Graylock; p. 39 AP Photo/Matt Sayles; p. 44 Elnur/Shutterstock; p. 48 Matt Richman

Printed in the United States of America

1 2 3 4 5 6 7 8 9 14 13 12 11 10 09

Contents

Words in the glossary appear in **bold** type the first time they are used in the text.

“Sharapova is the best thing that could have HAPPENED TO WOMEN’S TENNIS.”

—Martina Navratilova, tennis great

Sharapova is all smiles after winning the 2004 Wimbledon championship.

Chapter 1

Another Winner

Lindsay Davenport's mouth hung open. Maria Sharapova had just bashed another winner past her. Davenport was supposed to be the "heavy hitter" of women's tennis. But 17-year-old Sharapova was about to steal her crown. This was no ordinary **match**. The winner would move on to play for the Wimbledon championship.

Davenport had beaten Sharapova easily in the first **set**. But Sharapova beat Davenport in the second set in a thrilling **tiebreaker**. In the third and last set, Sharapova won 6–1.

A day later, Sharapova was the 2004 Wimbledon champion. A new star was born. "Sharapova is the best thing that could have happened to women's tennis," all-time great Martina Navratilova has said.

Attack Mode

Maria Sharapova is tall, strong, and fearless. She uses her body like a whip to send tennis balls screaming across the net. She attacks at all times. When she falls behind in a match, she seems to hit the ball even harder. Sharapova uses her long legs to reach shots that other players must lunge for.

An opponent who lets up even for an instant risks losing to Sharapova. She can quickly change a close match into an easy victory. This makes her a favorite of young tennis fans all over the world.

TRUE OR FALSE?

Sharapova is the tallest women's professional tennis player.

For answers, see page 46.

▼ **Sharapova uses her long legs to get to shots that other players might miss.**

All About Maria

Name: Maria Yuryevna Sharapova

Birth Date: April 19, 1987

Birthplace: Nyagan, Soviet Union

Height: 6 feet 2 inches (188 centimeters)

Weight: 130 pounds (59 kilograms)

Current Home: Bradenton, Florida

Family: Mother, Yelena, and father, Yuri

Service With a Smile

Despite being a fierce player, Sharapova has a friendly, easygoing nature. She has a wonderful smile that can light up a tennis stadium. When she steps up to the **baseline**, the smile leaves her face. She is all business.

Her greatest weapon is her serve. Sharapova wins many of her service games without losing a single point. Her serve has been clocked at more than 120 miles per hour (193 kilometers per hour).

"Maria has this ability to just raise the level of her game," says fellow Russian tennis player Nadia Petrova. "She can just defy everything and everybody . . . she wants to win so bad."

Fact File

Sharapova can "tie up" an opponent by aiming a serve right at her body. It is very hard for the player to return a serve while jumping out of the way!

▲ Sharapova doesn't hold back when she hits the ball.

Loudmouth

Sharapova is known for grunting loudly when she hits the ball. Scientific tests have shown that tennis players hit the ball harder when they exhale—and even harder when they grunt.

How loud is Sharapova? Players used to make the same complaint about Monica Seles, who dominated women's tennis during the early 1990s. Her grunt was once measured at 93 **decibels**. Decibels measure the power of a sound. Sharapova's grunt comes in at around 100 decibels. From a distance, a jet plane takeoff is 125 decibels.

TRUE OR FALSE?

Sharapova won ESPY awards as the top tennis player in 2005, 2007, and 2008.

From Russia With Love

Sharapova now lives in the United States. But she was born in what is now Russia and considers herself Russian. Since 2000, Russia has produced some of the best women's tennis players. They have shined in world competitions like the Olympics and Federation Cup. Russia's first true women's tennis star was Olga Morozova. In 1974, 13 years before Sharapova was born, Morozova reached the finals of both the French Open and Wimbledon.

Fact File

Maria Sharapova has always enjoyed cooking. She loves to read cookbooks.

Russian to Number One

Here is how Russian players have done in the women's tennis rankings.*

Player	Career	Highest Ranking*
Anna Chakvetadze	2003–present	5
Elena Dementieva	1998–present	4
Anna Kournikova	1995–2003	8
Svetlana Kuznetsova	2000–present	2
Olga Morozova	1966–1977	7
Anastasia Myskina	1998–present	2
Nadia Petrova	1999–present	3
Dinara Safina	2000–present	2
Maria Sharapova	2001–present	1
Vera Zvonareva	2000–present	9

*Through 2008

▼ **Elena Dementieva is one of many Russian tennis stars.**

“This girl is one of the most talented PLAYERS I HAVE EVER SEEN.”

—Yuri Udkin, Russian Tennis Federation coach

Maria’s father has helped and supported her career from the beginning.

Chapter 2
Courting Success

Maria Sharapova began her tennis journey in the Soviet Union. She was born in 1987, in the western part of Siberia. Siberia is part of Russia. Russia was the largest nation in the Soviet Union. The Soviet Union split up into several nations a few years after Sharapova was born.

Today, Russia is known for producing many top tennis players. Sharapova is probably the most famous. Back in the 1980s, however, the country was known more for its basketball and hockey teams. Its tennis program was still growing. Many people are amazed that Russia has come so far so fast in tennis. Sharapova's story may be the most amazing of all.

Fact File

Maria's family name is Sharapov. In Russia, many women add an "a" to their family name. That is why Maria's last name is Sharapova.

Meltdown

In a way, Maria Sharapova's story began a year before she was born. Her parents, Yelena and Yuri Sharapov, lived in the city of Gomel. Today, Gomel is part of the country of Belarus. In 1986, an accident occurred at a nuclear plant in the town of Chernobyl, about 80 miles (129 km) away from Gomel. Deadly amounts of **radiation** were released into the air.

At first, the government did not admit how bad the accident was. Yuri was an engineer, so he understood the danger. He and his wife moved far away to Nyagan, where Maria was born.

▼ When Maria was two, her family moved to Sochi. It is located on the Black Sea.

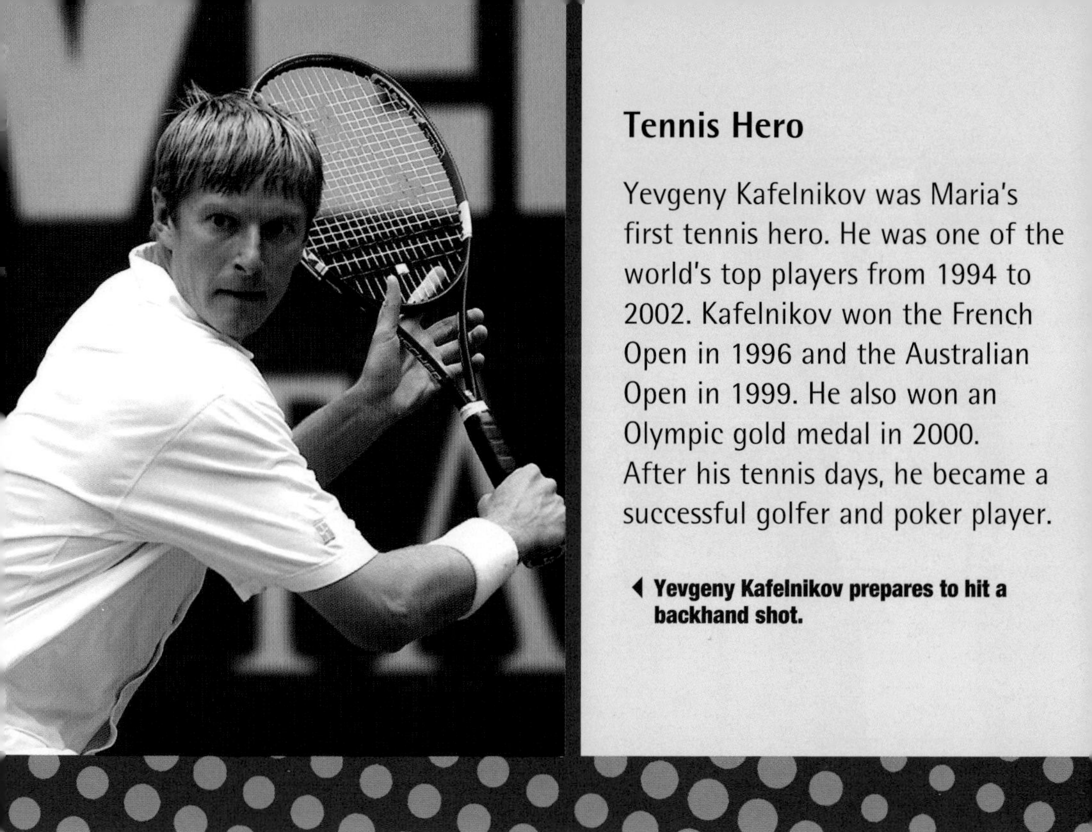

Tennis Hero

Yevgeny Kafelnikov was Maria's first tennis hero. He was one of the world's top players from 1994 to 2002. Kafelnikov won the French Open in 1996 and the Australian Open in 1999. He also won an Olympic gold medal in 2000. After his tennis days, he became a successful golfer and poker player.

◀ Yevgeny Kafelnikov prepares to hit a backhand shot.

Settling In

When Maria was two, her family moved again. They settled in Sochi, a quiet town on the coast of the Black Sea. They made many new friends. One of their friends was the father of tennis star Yevgeny Kafelnikov.

The two "tennis dads" often played together. Mr. Kafelnikov gave Maria one of his son's old rackets. The Sharapovs cut down the handle so she could swing the racket. She began playing at the age of four.

When Sharapova was a baby, her mother attended college and her father worked in the oil fields.

▲ **Maria attended a tennis clinic in Russia like this one.**

Strokes of Genius

Maria spent many hours each week playing and practicing. When she was not on a tennis court, she was whacking balls against the side of the family's house. By the age of six, Maria was the best young player in Sochi. Some tennis coaches urged Yuri to take his daughter to Moscow, the capital of Russia. They thought the Russian Tennis Federation would want to include her in its program.

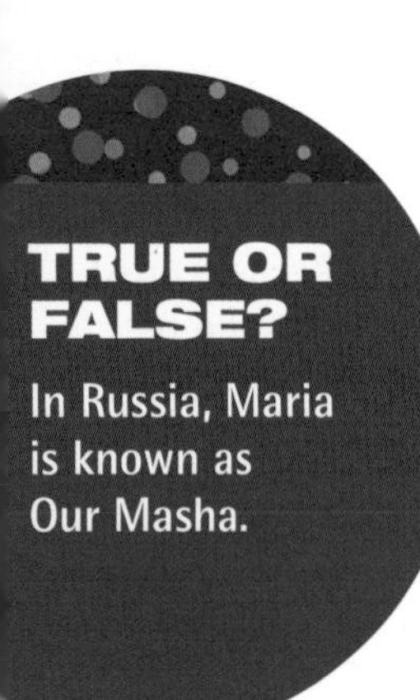

Martina & Me

Yuri Udkin was the coach of the Russian Tennis Federation. He watched six-year-old Maria swing her sawed-off racket and could not keep from smiling. "This girl is one of the most talented players I have ever seen," Udkin would say later.

Someone else who could spot talent was Martina Navratilova. She was one of the top players in the world. While playing matches in Moscow, Navratilova met Maria. Navratilova told the Sharapovs that Maria would get better training in the United States than in Russia.

Fact File

When Maria Sharapova returns to Russia to visit her grandparents, she brings rackets, clothes, and sneakers for her cousins and their tennis-playing friends.

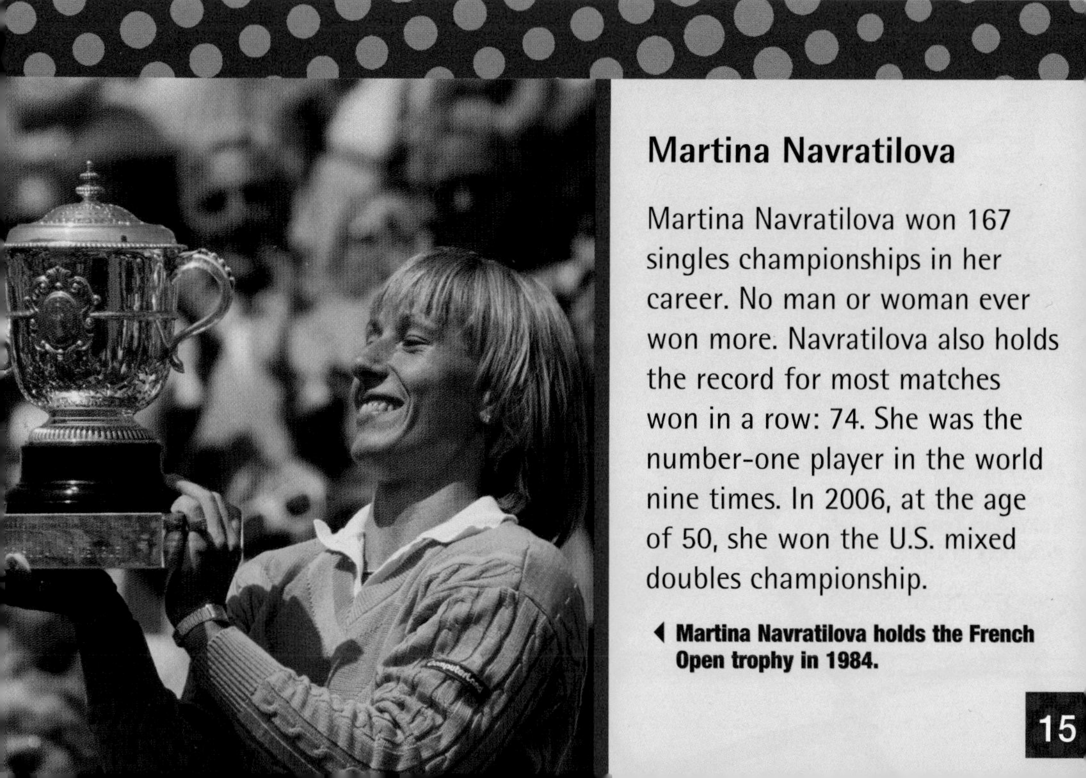

Martina Navratilova

Martina Navratilova won 167 singles championships in her career. No man or woman ever won more. Navratilova also holds the record for most matches won in a row: 74. She was the number-one player in the world nine times. In 2006, at the age of 50, she won the U.S. mixed doubles championship.

◀ Martina Navratilova holds the French Open trophy in 1984.

"She plays tennis like she's preparing FOR AN ATTACK, A BATTLE."

—Nick Bollettieri, coach

Maria takes a break at the Bollettieri Tennis Academy in 1998.

Chapter 3

Coming to America

Like all parents, the Sharapovs wanted the best for their child. They decided Maria should train at the Bollettieri Tennis Academy in Florida. To afford the trip, Maria's parents borrowed money from friends and family. Her father even took a dangerous job as a miner to make money. By the time Maria was seven, they had saved enough for two airline tickets, with about $1,000 left over.

To travel between countries, people often must get special permits called visas. Yuri and Maria were given visas, but Yelena was not. That meant Maria had to begin a new life in a strange country without her mom.

Nick's Place

TRUE OR FALSE?

Maria and Yuri were welcomed by the families of the other students at the Bollettieri Academy.

Nick Bollettieri had a gift for spotting talent in young athletes. He also knew how to turn young tennis players into top-ranked stars. This is one reason why tuition at the academy is very expensive.

Yuri had to work hard at different jobs to pay for Maria's training. Maria had to train hard to prove herself on the tennis court. Father and daughter grew very close during this time. Eventually, Maria showed enough promise to earn a scholarship to the academy. While she trained, she attended the local public school.

For young Maria, tennis was a priority. But she kept up with school, too.

Fame Game

Nick Bollettieri is famous for coaching some of the most successful tennis players in history. Here is how some of his best players did in their careers:

Player	Singles Titles
Andre Agassi	68
Monica Seles	53
Brian Gottfried	25
Jim Courier	23
Mary Pierce	18

◀ Monica Seles, here with the Australian Open trophy, was also a Bollettieri student.

Junior Achiever

Maria's game improved quickly. "She plays tennis like she's preparing for an attack, a battle. That's Maria Sharapova. There is no monkey business. Every shot has a purpose," Nick Bollettieri has said.

Bollettieri and other coaches at the academy could see that she would be a tall player. Even before she started growing, they taught her how to use her height to her advantage.

Fact File

Maria's first full-time tennis coach was Robert Lansdorp. He had coached champions Tracy Austin, Pete Sampras, and Lindsay Davenport.

Grand Slam

There are four major tennis tournaments each year. They are the Australian Open, the French Open, Wimbledon, and the U.S. Open. Together, they are known as the Grand Slam. During each Grand Slam, junior tournaments are held, too. These are for young players who are not yet ready to compete against the best players in the world.

Tournament	Location	Month	Surface
Australian Open	Melbourne	January	Hard
French Open	Paris	May/June	Clay
Wimbledon	London	June/July	Grass
U.S. Open	New York	Aug/Sept	Hard

Young Pro

When Sharapova turned 14, she decided to declare herself a professional. That meant she could earn prize money at tournaments. She could also receive money for **endorsing** rackets and shoes.

Sharapova entered the junior tournaments at the Australian Open and Wimbledon in 2002. She reached the **semifinals** of each. This was a great achievement for such a young player. Later in 2002, Sharapova won three minor tournaments playing against adults. At the end of the year, she was ranked number 186 in the world.

In 2003, 16-year-old Sharapova was the youngest winner on the women's tennis tour.

Making Progress

In 2003, Sharapova had a wonderful year. She stunned the fans at Wimbledon by beating three top players—and almost reaching the quarterfinals. Later in the year, she won her first two singles championships as a pro. She finished the year ranked number 32.

TRUE OR FALSE?

In April 2004, Sharapova was one of six Russian women ranked in the top 20.

She continued to improve in 2004. In June, she won a tournament in Birmingham, England. The event was played on grass. Sharapova's long arms and legs and her powerful serve gave her an advantage on this slick, fast surface.

▸ **Sharapova celebrates a winning moment at the 2003 Wimbledon tournament.**

"My next goal is to be NUMBER ONE IN THE WORLD."

—Maria Sharapova, 2004

Sharapova

Chapter 4

Aiming for Number One

Sharapova was 17 years old in the summer of 2004. She stood 6 feet 2 inches (188 cm) tall and had tremendous strength. People had already started to notice her for her good looks and elegant style off the court. Now she was giving them a reason to watch her on the court. She had a hard serve and an **aggressive** style. She was learning from her victories as well as her defeats. This is the mark of a champion.

In 2004, Sharapova said, "My next goal is to be number one in the world." Yet few in the tennis world thought she would rise to the top of the rankings. There were just too many other players with equal talent and more experience. Sharapova would soon prove the experts wrong.

Miracle on Grass

Maria Sharapova's name was still unknown to most tennis fans watching the 2004 Wimbledon tournament. She had just won a tournament on grass in Birmingham. Even so, no one thought she could actually win Wimbledon at age 17.

Sharapova gained confidence by winning her first three matches easily. She struggled against Ai Sugiyama and Amy Frazier in the next two rounds, but won each. That set up the incredible victory over Lindsay Davenport in the semifinals.

TRUE OR FALSE?

Sharapova was the first Russian to win a singles title at Wimbledon.

▼ **Sharapova hugs her father after winning the 2004 Wimbledon championship.**

▲ Sharapova shares a moment with Serena Williams as they hold their Wimbledon trophies.

Big Surprise

Sharapova's victory over Serena Williams in was one of the most surprising in Wimbledon history. Williams had won six Grand Slam titles and 20 matches in a row on grass when she and Sharapova met in the Wimbledon final. In 2002, Williams won Wimbledon without losing a set throughout the tournament. She beat her sister Venus in the final.

Suddenly Serena

Sharapova's head was still spinning after she beat Davenport. Suddenly, she realized that her opponent in the finals was Serena Williams. They had played once before, and Williams had destroyed Sharapova.

In that meeting, Williams had won many points on Sharapova's **second serve**. This time, Sharapova hit her second serve as hard as she could. Sharapova won the first set 6–1. The second set was much closer. But Sharapova outlasted Williams, 6–4, to win her first Grand Slam. "She's kind of like me," Williams said after the match. "She doesn't back off."

Fact File

Sharapova was the third-youngest player to win Wimbledon since the tournament began in 1877.

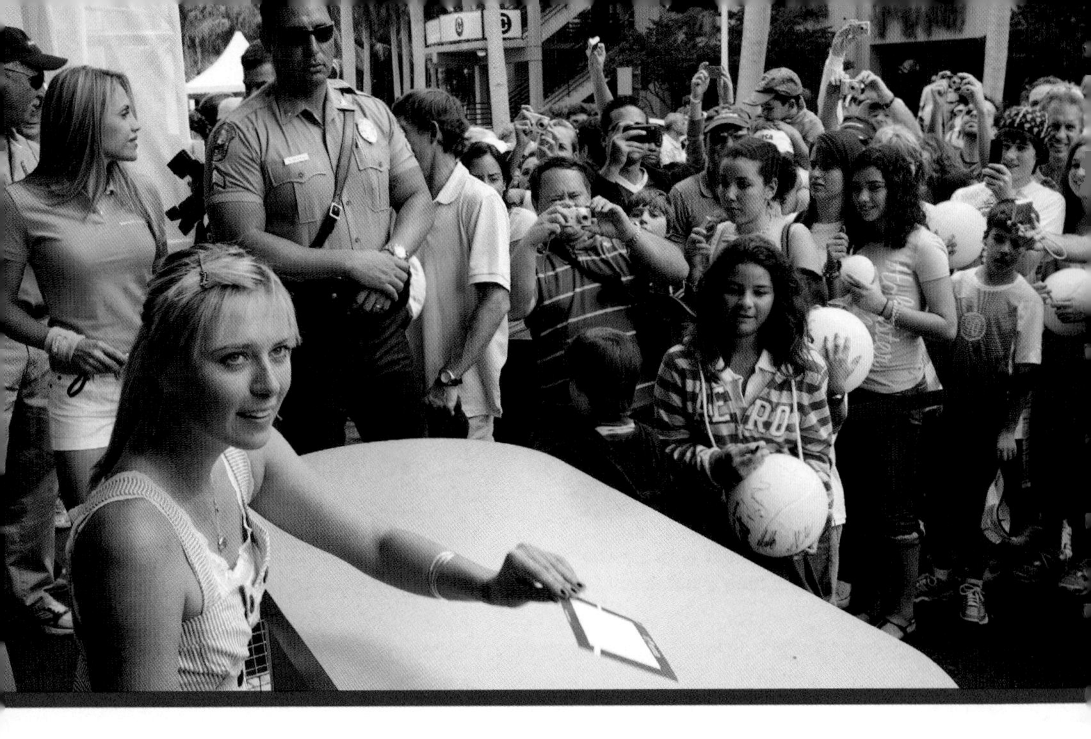

▲ Sharapova signs autographs at a tennis tournament in Florida.

The Face of Tennis

After winning Wimbledon, Sharapova became the most famous person in her sport. Her face was on the cover of magazines. Fans mobbed her. It was a lot for a teenager to deal with. Playing tennis was almost a relief. "When I walk through the gate to the court, that's my escape," she explains. "I block out everything."

Sharapova became a target for other players, who worked extra hard to beat her in 2005. Still, Sharapova did well enough to earn the number-one ranking. She held it for one week in August and six weeks in September and October.

Fact File

In 2004, terrorists attacked a school in the Russian town of Beslan. Sharapova donated money to victims of the attack.

"I Love New York"

The wear and tear of tennis was starting to take its toll on Sharapova. She had sore legs and a sore shoulder. She had to sit out several tournaments in 2006. When she was healthy, she continued her fine play.

Sharapova's two biggest rivals that year were Amelie Mauresmo and Justine Henin. At the U.S. Open, Sharapova faced Mauresmo in the semifinals and Henin in the finals. She beat both of them to capture her second Grand Slam. Soon after, Sharapova met Henin in the last match of the season. Maria lost the match and finished 2006 ranked just behind Henin.

TRUE OR FALSE?

Sharapova loves reading the Twilight series by Stephenie Meyer.

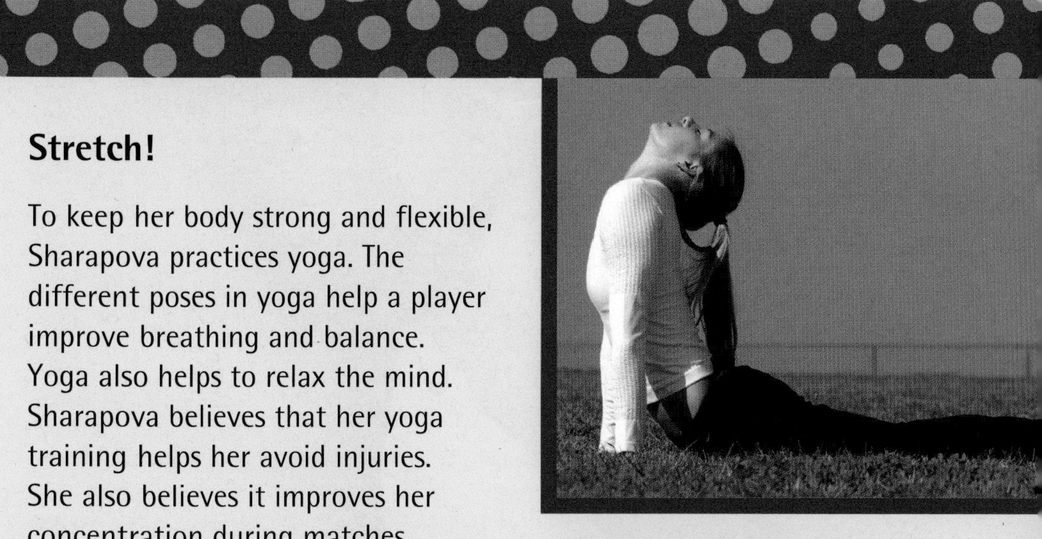

Stretch!

To keep her body strong and flexible, Sharapova practices yoga. The different poses in yoga help a player improve breathing and balance. Yoga also helps to relax the mind. Sharapova believes that her yoga training helps her avoid injuries. She also believes it improves her concentration during matches.

▲ **Sharapova uses yoga to stay strong, flexible, and relaxed.**

"Sometimes people play their best tennis when THEY DON'T EXPECT THEIR BEST TENNIS TO COME OUT."

—Maria Sharapova

Sharapova waves to the crowd after a match at the 2007 Australian Open.

Chapter 5

Wonder Down Under

Australians often refer to their country as "Down Under," because it is located "under" the equator. The Australian Open starts in January, which is summer in Australia. So the weather can be very hot.

In 2007, Sharapova reached the Australian Open finals. She again faced Serena Williams. Williams had been slowed down by injuries, and her ranking had sunk to number 81. But Williams won the match.

Sharapova was angry with herself but was gracious in defeat. "Sometimes people play their best tennis when they don't expect their best tennis to come out," she said of Serena's win. Sharapova began thinking about the Australian Open in 2008.

Tough Year

Sharapova played hard in 2007 but had little to show for it. Her shoulder ached for much of the year. This reduced the speed of her serve, her best weapon. Her lowest moment came at the U.S. Open. She lost to an unknown 18-year-old. Sharapova served a dozen **double faults** and committed 49 **unforced errors**.

In her last match of 2007, she met Henin again. They played for almost three and a half hours in the finals of the Sony Ericsson Championship. It was one of the longest finals ever in women's tennis. Sharapova lost the match but felt strong heading into 2008.

TRUE OR FALSE?

Sharapova's second serve has been clocked at more than 100 mph (160 kph).

Sharapova's serve is key to her playing a good match.

Eye on Yuri

Maria's biggest fan is her father, Yuri. He is easy to spot at matches. He moves around nervously, and sometimes is noisy. Other players get annoyed by this behavior. They believe he is trying to help Maria win. No coaching is allowed from the stands. Tournament officials have warned Yuri several times not to signal his daughter or give her advice.

Yuri Sharapov is devoted to his daughter and her tennis success.

Undefeated!

Sharapova arrived at the 2008 Australian Open more focused than ever. With so many great players in the tournament, she could not afford to have a bad day.

Sharapova defeated Davenport and Henin in the early rounds. Then she beat Jelena Jankovic in the semifinals. In the finals, she faced Ana Ivanovic. Sharapova won a close first set, 7–5. She had an easier time in the second set, winning 6–3. Sharapova had won her third Grand Slam. During the entire tournament, she did not lose a set.

Fact File

Sharapova lost only 10 points on her serve in the 2008 Australian Open final.

▲ Sharapova hugs a teammate after the Russian team's victory over Israel in 2008.

The Federation Cup

The Federation Cup is a competition among women's teams from different countries. It is played throughout the year. Each competition takes place over three days. There are two singles matches the first day, a doubles match the second day, and two more singles matches on the final day. The first team to take three matches wins.

Country Girl

Sharapova has lived in the United States since she was seven years old. She speaks perfect English. Still, she is a Russian citizen and considers herself Russian.

Sharapova had wanted to join Russia's Federation Cup team for many years. For one reason or another, she had never been able to do this. Finally, in 2008, she did and took the court for Russia against Israel. Sharapova won both of her singles matches to lead her country to victory.

Fact File

The Davis Cup is a competition among men's teams from different countries. It is similar to the women's Federation Cup.

Lady in Waiting

After winning the Australian Open, Sharapova's old injuries came back. She lost the number-one ranking to Henin. That spring, Sharapova had to pull out of an event in Florida. This was bad news for her and the tournament. Thousands of fans had bought tickets hoping to see her play.

Days later, Sharapova got some good news. She heard that Henin had decided to quit tennis. That meant Sharapova —who was ranked number two—was now the top-ranked player in tennis once again. She would have preferred to "take" the number-one ranking from Henin with a victory on the court. Still, Sharapova was proud of this achievement.

TRUE OR FALSE?

At Wimbledon in 2008, Sharapova surprised the crowd by wearing long pants instead of a dress.

Former number-one player Justine Henin retired from the game in 2008.

"When you're going through tough moments,

YOU NEVER KNOW WHEN YOU'RE GOING TO HAVE GOOD MOMENTS."

—Maria Sharapova

Sharapova teaches a tennis clinic in New Haven, Connecticut.

Chapter 6
New Challenges

The mark of a tennis champion is not just how well she wears her crown. It is also how she responds to challenges. Sometimes these challenges are right across the net. Sometimes they happen where no one can see them—inside the body and mind. "When you're going through tough moments, you never know when you're going to have good moments," Sharapova has said.

Sharapova has shown again and again that she will work hard to overcome any obstacle. Few champions have come so far so fast, and shown they have what it takes to stay at the top of the game. Some of Sharapova's toughest challenges came in 2008 and 2009—just when it looked like everything was about to go her way.

Fact File

Doctors used a test called an MRI to discover Sharapova's injury. MRIs let doctors get a good view of injuries inside the body.

Sore Spot

Sharapova's number-one ranking did not last long. At the 2008 French Open, she lost an early round match to Dinara Safina. The loss bumped Sharapova out of the top spot. Worse, she reinjured her shoulder during the match.

In the past, Sharapova knew how to cure her shoulder problems. She used a combination of exercise and rest. This time, nothing seemed to work.

▼ A trainer works on Sharapova's injured shoulder.

Maria's Favorites

- ✔ **Foods:** Russian and Thai
- ✔ **Dessert:** French crepes with Nutella
- ✔ **Junk Food:** Snickers bars
- ✔ **Movies:** Romance and comedy
- ✔ **Books:** Sherlock Holmes mysteries and *Pippi Longstocking*
- ✔ **Drink:** Orangina

Doctors' Orders

After losing in the second round at Wimbledon, Sharapova began to worry more about her shoulder. Doctors tested her shoulder and discovered a small tear. The tear had not been there in the spring.

Sharapova faced a difficult choice. The damage was to her **rotator cuff**. This is an injury that affects baseball pitchers and football quarterbacks. In Sharapova's case, the tear could repair itself with a few months of rest. An operation might keep her off the court for almost a year. Sharapova decided to rest. She returned to tennis after the Australian Open in 2009.

Fact File

Sharapova was named a Goodwill Ambassador by the United Nations during the 2007 season.

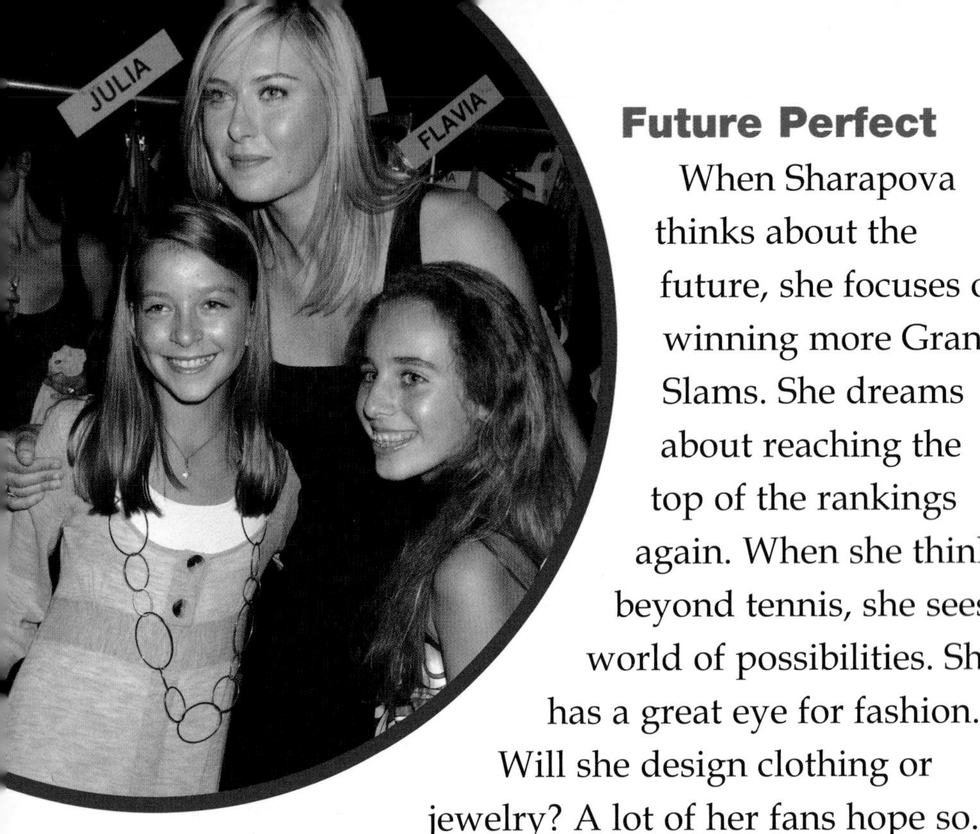

▲ **Sharapova poses with young fans at a fashion show in New York City.**

Future Perfect

When Sharapova thinks about the future, she focuses on winning more Grand Slams. She dreams about reaching the top of the rankings again. When she thinks beyond tennis, she sees a world of possibilities. She has a great eye for fashion. Will she design clothing or jewelry? A lot of her fans hope so.

Sharapova already has almost everything a young woman could want. Whatever she does in the years to come, she wants to make a difference. She has heard the roar of the crowd. She has cashed huge paychecks. Sharapova wants to know that she matters in the real world the way she does in the tennis world.

"No matter how much money I'm making, what I've done in my career, no matter what cool cars or house I have, I'm still Maria," she says. "I'm still a normal girl who enjoys life."

Fact File

Sharapova has her own charity, the Maria Sharapova Foundation. It helps kids reach their dreams.

Making a Difference

As a tennis player, Sharapova visits more than two dozen cities a year. At each stop, she makes sure to help local charities. She knows that her name and her face can help raise money.

Maria Sharapova enjoys working with children. She knows that she was lucky to find tennis at such a young age. She wants other kids to be able to follow their dreams. It doesn't matter whether those young people hope for a career in athletics, science, education, or the arts. Sharapova contributes to the charities that can make their dreams come true.

TRUE OR FALSE?

Sharapova designed a tennis bracelet for the jeweler Tiffany & Co.

▼ Sharapova is a big fan of actor Orlando Bloom.

Wish List

On her web site, Sharapova says these are the people she would most like to meet for a cup of coffee:

- ✔ **Marilyn Monroe** (actress)
- ✔ **Orlando Bloom** (actor)
- ✔ **Marc Jacobs** (clothing designer)
- ✔ **Gwyneth Paltrow** (actress)

Time Line

1987 Maria Sharapova is born on April 19 in Nyagan, Soviet Union.

1994 Maria and her father move to the United States. Maria begins training at the Nick Bollettieri Tennis Academy.

2001 Sharapova becomes a professional player.

2003 Sharapova wins her first pro singles title.

2004 Sharapova defeats Serena Williams to win Wimbledon.

2005 Sharapova becomes the first Russian player to be ranked number one in the world.

2006 Sharapova wins the U.S. Open.

2007 Sharapova is named Goodwill Ambassador to the United Nations Development Programme.

2008 Sharapova wins the Australian Open. She and the Russian team win the Federation Cup.

Glossary

aggressive: bold, energetic, and extremely competitive

baseline: the "back line" on a tennis court. A server is not allowed to step across this line until the ball is struck.

decibels: the measurement used to show how loud a noise is

double faults: points lost by the server when neither the first nor the second serve goes in

endorsing: supporting or approving products or services

match: a meeting between two players. In women's tennis, a match usually lasts until one player has won two sets.

radiation: a type of energy that can be poisonous to living things

rotator cuff: a group of muscles that holds the shoulder in place

second serve: the serve attempted after a player's first serve is unsuccessful. A second serve is usually slower than a first serve, which makes it easier to return.

semifinals: the round before the finals. The winners of semifinal matches meet in the final to decide the championship.

set: a unit of scoring in tennis. The first player to win six games (by two games) wins a set.

tiebreaker: a scoring rule used when the score in a set is 6–6. Most tiebreakers last until one player has won seven points.

unforced errors: points lost by a player through physical mistakes or poor judgment

To Find Out More

Books

Glaser, Jason. *Maria Sharapova*. New York: PowerKids Press, 2008.

Sapet, Kerrily. *Maria Sharapova*. Broomall, PA: Mason Crest Publishers, 2009.

Savage, Jeff. *Maria Sharapova*. Minneapolis: Lerner Publications, 2008.

Williams, Venus, and Serena Williams. *How to Play Tennis*. New York: DK Children's Publishing, 2004.

Web Sites

Children of Chernobyl Foundation
www.cofcsd.org
This site contains information about Sharapova's charity work.

Maria Sharapova
www.mariasharapova.com
Sharapova's official web site has a question-and-answer feature and information on her foundations.

Women's Tennis Association
www.wtatour.com
Here you can find a bio page on Sharapova and up-to-date statistics and tournament results.

Publisher's note to educators and parents: Our editors have carefully reviewed these web sites to ensure that they are suitable for children. Many web sites change frequently, however, and we cannot guarantee that a site's future contents will continue to meet our high standards of quality and educational value. Be advised that children should be closely supervised whenever they access the Internet.

Championships*

Wimbledon Champion
2004

U.S. Open Champion
2006

Australian Open Champion
2008

Federation Cup Championship Team
2008

*As of March 2009

Source Notes

p. 5 Matt Butler, "She's the best thing," *Sunday Mirror*, June 19, 2005.

p. 7 Liz Robbins, "Biggest Distraction for Sharapova Is Her Father," *New York Times*, September 9, 2005.

p. 15 "Maria Sharapova," Black Book Partners, www.jockbio.com/Bios/Sharapova/Sharapova_quotes.html.

p. 19 Greg Boeck, "Russian's Game a Thing of Beauty," *USA Today*, January 12, 2004.

p. 23 "Match Girl," *People*, July 19, 2004.

p. 26 Dennis Passa, "Sharapova impressive after third Grand Slam singles win," AP Online, January 26, 2008.

p. 29 Dennis Passa, "Sharapova vs. Serena a Replay of 2005," AP Online, January 25, 2007.

p. 35 "Sharapova matches court brilliance with heartfelt victory speech," *Sunday Gazette-Mail*, January 27, 2008.

p. 38 Liz Robbins, "At 19, Sharapova Is Rich, Famous and, Ahem, Normal," *New York Times*, September 11, 2006.

True or False Answers

Page 6 False. Akgul Amanmuradova of Uzbekistan is 6 feet 3 inches (191 cm), 1 inch taller than Sharapova.

Page 8 True.

Page 14 True.

Page 18 False. The other families saw Maria as an "outsider" who might be taking the place of a talented American child.

Page 21 True.

Page 24 True.

Page 27 True.

Page 30 True.

Page 33 False. She surprised everyone by wearing tennis shorts.

Page 39 True.

Young Maria had a hard adjustment to the Bollettieri Academy.

Sharapova was the first Russian player to win a Wimbledon singles title.

Index

About the Author

Mark Stewart has written more than 200 nonfiction books for schools and libraries, including biographies of tennis stars Pete Sampras, Venus and Serena Williams, and Monica Seles. Mark was the editor of *RACQUET* magazine in the 1980s and 1990s, and became friendly with many of the tennis stars from that era. He also coauthored a tennis instruction book with Nick Bollettieri.